Don't Start a Business

Buy One

Outsmart the Startup Game with a Complete Guide to Business Acquisition for Beginners

By Elisabeth Miazello

Copyright

© 2024 Elisabeth Miazello. All Rights Reserved.

This eBook is protected by U.S. and international copyright laws. No part may be reproduced, distributed, or transmitted in any form or by any means without the author's written permission, except for brief quotes in reviews or non-commercial uses allowed by copyright law.

Disclaimer

This eBook provides general information in good faith. We make no guarantees about the accuracy, reliability, or completeness of the content. Use of this eBook is at your own risk, and we are not liable for any losses or damages resulting from its use.

Dear Valued Reader,

Thank you for purchasing **"Don't Start a Business, Buy One"**! Your decision to invest in this eBook is the first step towards achieving your entrepreneurial dreams. We're thrilled to have you on this journey and are confident that you'll find the insights and strategies in this book both inspiring and actionable.

In this eBook, you'll learn:

The Essentials of Business Acquisition, Finding the Perfect Business, Evaluating Potential Purchases, Effective Communication with Sellers, Financing Your Purchase, Managing and Growing Your Business and Real-Life Success Stories.

We hope you enjoy reading this eBook and that it provides you with the knowledge and confidence to take your next big step. If you have any questions or need further assistance, please don't hesitate to reach out.

Thank you again for your purchase. Here's to your success!

Best regards,
Elisabeth Miazello

Author Page

P.S. Don't forget to leave a review and share your thoughts on how this eBook has helped you!

Ready to Transform Your Future?

Grab your **FREE eBook** now and discover:

7 Businesses to Avoid and 4 Winning Opportunities: Your Business Success Guide.

Don't miss out on this opportunity to kickstart your entrepreneurial journey!

Scan the **QR Code** Above or Visit IRNOX.com/7c for an Instant Free Download

Take the first step towards financial freedom.

Table of Contents:

Introduction _____ 6

Understanding the Basics _____ 9

Mindset and Preparation _____ 12

Finding Businesses to Buy _____ 15

Evaluating Business Opportunities _____ 18

Approaching Business Owners _____ 22

Financing Your Purchase _____ 26

Due Diligence Process _____ 30

Closing the Deal _____ 34

Case Studies and Success Stories _____ 38

Building and Growing Your Acquired Business ____ 42

Overcoming Challenges _____ 46

Resources and Tools _____ 50

Recap of Key Points _____ 54

Introduction

Why Buying a Business is a Great Way to Build Wealth

You've probably heard that the best way to get rich is to start your own business. But here's a little secret: you don't have to come up with a brilliant idea to become wealthy. Many of the richest people on the Forbes 500 list didn't start their own companies from scratch—they bought existing businesses. Buying a business allows you to start making money from day one without the high risks associated with startups. It's a proven path to financial freedom and long-term wealth.

Common Myths About Business Ownership

There are a lot of misconceptions out there about owning a business. Let's debunk a few of them:

Myth 1: You Need a Lot of Money to Buy a Business.
Truth: There are plenty of ways to finance a business purchase, including seller financing, loans, and even leveraging your skills and expertise.

Myth 2: Only Experts Can Run a Business Successfully.
Truth: You don't need to be a business genius. With the right mindset, strategies, and support, anyone can learn to run a business.

Myth 3: Finding a Good Business to Buy is Impossible.
Truth: There are more businesses for sale than you might think, especially with many baby boomers retiring. With the right tactics, you can find a great opportunity.

Overview of the eBook Structure

In this eBook, we're going to take you step-by-step through the process of buying a business. Here's what you can expect:

1. **Understanding the Basics**: We'll cover what business acquisition is and why it's often better than starting from scratch.

2. **Mindset** and **Preparation**: Learn how to develop the right mindset and set clear goals for your journey.

3. **Finding Businesses to Buy**: Discover the best channels and strategies for finding businesses that are for sale.

4. **Evaluating Business Opportunities**: We'll guide you on how to assess a business's value and potential through financial documents and market analysis.

5. **Approaching Business Owners**: Learn effective communication and negotiation tactics to make your offer stand out.

6. **Financing Your Purchase**: Explore different financing options and creative strategies to fund your business acquisition.

7. **Due Diligence Process**: Understand how to thoroughly investigate a business before making a final decision.

8. **Closing the Deal**: Steps to finalize the purchase and smoothly transition into ownership.

9. **Case Studies** and **Success Stories**: Get inspired by real-life examples of successful business acquisitions.

10. **Building** and **Growing Your Acquired Business**: Tips and strategies for managing and growing your new business.

11. **Overcoming Challenges**: Advice on dealing with setbacks and maintaining motivation.

12. **Resources** and **Tools**: A list of recommended books, websites, templates, and support groups to help you on your journey.

By the end of this eBook, you'll have all the knowledge and tools you need to confidently buy and run a successful business. Let's get started on this exciting journey to business ownership and wealth building!

Understanding the Basics

What is Business Acquisition?

Business acquisition is simply the process of buying an existing business. Instead of starting a business from scratch, you purchase one that's already up and running. This can include buying a small local shop, a franchise, or even a large company. The goal is to take over the operations, grow the business, and reap the rewards without having to go through the risky and often lengthy startup phase.

Benefits of Buying Over Starting a Business

1. **Immediate Cash Flow**: When you buy a business, you start making money from day one. There's no need to wait months or years to see a return on your investment.

2. **Established Customer Base**: The business already has customers who know and trust it. You don't have to spend time and money building a brand from scratch.

3. **Proven Business Model**: The business has a track record, so you know it works. You can analyze its financial history to make informed decisions.

4. **Easier Financing**: Lenders are often more willing to finance the purchase of an existing

business with a proven track record than a brand-new startup.

5. **Lower Risk**: Starting a new business is risky—many fails within the first few years. Buying an established business reduces this risk significantly.

Key Concepts and Terminology

1. **Due Diligence**: This is the thorough investigation you conduct before buying a business. It involves reviewing financial records, operations, legal matters, and more to ensure you know exactly what you're getting into.

2. **Seller Financing**: This is when the seller of the business agrees to finance part of the purchase price. Instead of paying the full amount upfront, you make regular payments to the seller over time.

3. **Cash Flow**: The amount of money moving in and out of the business. Positive cash flow means the business earns more than it spends, which is crucial for its sustainability.

4. **Balance Sheet**: A financial statement that provides a snapshot of a business's assets, liabilities, and owner's equity at a specific point in time. It helps you understand the financial health of the business.

5. **Profit** and **Loss Statement** (P&L): Also known as an income statement, this document shows the company's revenues, costs, and expenses over a period. It's essential for assessing profitability.

6. **Valuation**: The process of determining how much a business is worth. This can be based on earnings, assets, market conditions, and other factors.

7. **Non-Disclosure Agreement** (NDA): A legal contract that ensures confidentiality. It's often used during the due diligence phase to protect sensitive information shared by the seller.

8. **Acquisition Strategy**: Your plan for buying and integrating a business. It includes how you'll find businesses, evaluate them, negotiate the purchase, and manage the transition.

Understanding these basics sets the foundation for your journey into business acquisition. Armed with this knowledge, you'll be better prepared to navigate the process and make smart, informed decisions. Let's dive deeper and explore each aspect in detail to ensure you're ready to become a successful business owner.

Mindset and Preparation

Developing the Right Mindset

Before you can successfully buy a business, you need to get your head in the right place. The number one killer of business dreams is the wrong mindset. If you're stuck in negative thinking, you won't make offers, do the work, or take the necessary risks. Believe that you can do this! If you're not lazy and willing to learn, you can buy a business.

Overcoming Common Fears and Misconceptions

It's natural to have doubts. Let's tackle some of the big ones:

- "Can I really buy a business?" Absolutely. Most people can, as long as they're committed and willing to learn.

- "Can I leave my job?" Yes, you can transition from your W2 job to owning a business. Many successful entrepreneurs did exactly that.

- "I've never run a business before. Do I have what it takes?" Maybe. Stick with this guide, and you'll find out. Key traits include hard work, curiosity, resilience, and a willingness to learn and adapt.

Setting Clear Goals and Objectives

To succeed, you need a clear plan. Here's how to set your goals:

1. **Define What You Want**: Know exactly what you want from this journey. Do you want financial freedom, more time with family, or the challenge of growing a business?

2. **Embrace Risk** and **Courage**: Accept that there will be tough times. True entrepreneurship involves risk and sometimes finding yourself in difficult situations. Stay resilient and push through.

3. **Get Creative**: Buying a business is a creative way to build wealth. Think outside the box and find innovative solutions to obstacles.

4. **Stay Optimistic**: Optimists get rich; pessimists sound smart but often achieve less. Keep a positive outlook and focus on the potential rewards.

5. **Continuous Learning**: Never stop learning. The more you know, the better equipped you'll be to handle challenges and seize opportunities.

6. **Know Your 'Why'**: Have a compelling vision that keeps you motivated. Whether it's escaping a job you hate or achieving a dream lifestyle, keep your 'why' at the forefront.

7. **Adaptability** and **Patience**: Be ready to pivot when necessary and have the patience to see things through. Success doesn't come overnight.

Developing the right mindset and preparing yourself mentally is crucial. Once you're ready mentally, you'll be equipped to handle the practical steps of buying a business. Stay focused, stay positive, and keep pushing forward. Your dream of owning a business is within reach!

Finding Businesses to Buy

Exploring Different Channels (Online Marketplaces, Local Networks)

So, where do you start looking for businesses to buy? There are a few key channels to explore:

1. **Online Marketplaces**: Websites like BizBuySell, BizQuest, and Flippa are great places to start. These platforms list businesses for sale, complete with financial details and contact information for the sellers. You can browse by industry, location, and price range to find a business that fits your criteria.

2. **Local Networks**: Sometimes, the best opportunities are right in your own backyard. Attend local business events, join your Chamber of Commerce, and network with other entrepreneurs. Local accountants, lawyers, and business brokers can also be valuable resources. They often know about businesses that are for sale before they hit the public market.

3. **Business Brokers**: Brokers specialize in connecting buyers with sellers. They can help you find businesses that match your interests and financial capacity. While they charge a fee, their expertise and connections can be worth the investment.

16

Utilizing Social Media for Deal Flow

Social media isn't just for keeping up with friends—it's a powerful tool for finding business opportunities:

1. **LinkedIn**: Optimize your profile to highlight your interest in buying businesses. Make it clear that you're in the market, and post updates about your acquisition journey. Join LinkedIn groups focused on business buying and entrepreneurship. Reach out to business owners directly; many are open to conversations about selling.

2. **Facebook**: Believe it or not, Facebook is a goldmine for finding businesses. Many small business owners are active on Facebook, and you can join local business groups to see what's for sale. Also, consider running targeted ads to reach business owners who might be looking to sell.

3. **Twitter** and **Instagram**: Follow industry leaders, join conversations about business acquisitions, and use hashtags like #BusinessForSale or #Entrepreneur. Share your intent to buy a business and engage with others in the business community.

Leveraging Personal Networks and Professional Connections

Your existing network can be a treasure trove of business opportunities. Here's how to tap into it:

1. **Friends** and **Family**: Let everyone know you're looking to buy a business. You'd be surprised how many people know someone who's thinking about selling. Personal connections can lead to great deals that aren't publicly advertised.

2. **Professional Contacts**: Reach out to accountants, lawyers, and financial advisors. These professionals often have clients looking to sell their businesses. They can provide introductions and valuable insights into potential opportunities.

3. **Industry Contacts**: If you're interested in a specific industry, network with professionals in that field. Attend industry conferences, join trade associations, and engage with industry-specific online forums. People in your industry are more likely to hear about businesses for sale and can provide insider information.

By exploring these channels, utilizing social media, and leveraging your personal and professional networks, you'll increase your chances of finding a business that's the perfect fit for you. Stay proactive, keep your eyes and ears open, and don't be afraid to put yourself out there. Your dream business is out there waiting for you to find it!

Evaluating Business Opportunities

Key Financial Documents to Understand

Before diving into a business purchase, you need to get cozy with a few key financial documents. They'll give you a clear picture of the business's health and help you make an informed decision.

1. **Profit** and **Loss Statement** (P&L): This document shows the company's revenues, costs, and expenses over a specific period. It's crucial for understanding how much money the business is making or losing. Look for consistent revenue, controlled costs, and a healthy net profit.

2. **Balance Sheet**: This provides a snapshot of the business's financial position at a specific point in time. It lists assets, liabilities, and owner's equity. Key points to check are the company's liquidity (ability to pay off short-term obligations) and solvency (ability to meet long-term debts).

3. **Cash Flow Statement**: Cash is king. This statement shows the flow of cash in and out of the business. Positive cash flow indicates the business can cover its expenses and invest in growth. Pay special attention to cash flow from operations, as it reflects the core business activities.

Assessing Business Value and Potential

Evaluating a business isn't just about crunching numbers. You need to look at the bigger picture to assess its true value and growth potential.

1. **Revenue** and **Profit Trends**: Look at the historical performance. Are revenues and profits growing, stable, or declining? Consistent growth is a good sign, while fluctuations might indicate underlying issues.

2. **Customer Base**: A diverse and loyal customer base is a strong asset. If a business relies heavily on a few customers, it's riskier. Check for customer satisfaction and retention rates.

3. **Competitive Position**: Understand the business's position in the market. Who are its main competitors? Does it have a unique selling proposition (USP) or competitive advantage? A strong market position can be a significant growth driver.

4. **Operational Efficiency**: Evaluate the efficiency of business operations. Are there processes in place to ensure smooth running? Can you identify areas for cost savings or productivity improvements? Efficient operations contribute to higher profitability.

5. **Growth Opportunities**: Identify potential areas for growth. Can you expand the product line, enter new markets, or increase marketing efforts? Businesses with clear growth opportunities are more valuable.

Understanding Industry and Market Trends

To fully grasp a business's potential, you need to understand the broader industry and market trends. Here's how:

1. **Market Size** and **Growth**: Is the market for the business's products or services growing, stable, or shrinking? A growing market offers more opportunities for expansion and profitability.

2. **Industry Trends**: Stay informed about the latest trends and developments in the industry. Are there technological advancements, regulatory changes, or shifts in consumer behavior that could impact the business? Being ahead of the curve can provide a competitive edge.

3. **Competitive Landscape**: Analyze the level of competition. Is the market saturated, or is there room for new entrants? Understanding the competitive dynamics helps in assessing the business's ability to sustain and grow its market share.

4. **Economic Factors**: Consider the broader economic environment. Factors like interest rates, inflation, and economic cycles can influence business performance. A business that can withstand economic fluctuations is a safer bet.

By mastering these key financial documents, assessing the business's value and potential, and understanding the industry and market trends, you'll be well-equipped to make smart, informed decisions. Evaluating a business opportunity thoroughly ensures that you invest your time, money, and energy into a venture that's primed for success.

Approaching Business Owners

Effective Communication Strategies

When it comes to buying a business, how you communicate can make all the difference. Here's how to get it right:

1. **Be Clear** and **Direct**: Start with a straightforward message. Let the owner know that you're interested in buying their business. Avoid beating around the bush—clarity builds trust.

2. **Listen Actively**: Show genuine interest in what the owner has to say. Listening is key to understanding their motivations and concerns. Ask open-ended questions to get them talking about their business.

3. **Be Professional** and **Polite**: Approach the conversation with respect and professionalism. Use proper language, and be polite even if the initial response is not what you hoped for.

4. **Show Appreciation**: Acknowledge the hard work the owner has put into building their business. A little appreciation goes a long way in establishing a positive connection.

Building Rapport with Potential Sellers

Building a relationship with the seller is crucial. Here's how to create a strong rapport:

1. **Find Common Ground**: Look for shared interests or experiences. This could be anything from a mutual acquaintance to a common hobby. Finding common ground helps in establishing a personal connection.

2. **Be Honest** and **Transparent**: Sellers appreciate honesty. Be open about your intentions and your ability to close the deal. Transparency builds trust and can make the negotiation process smoother.

3. **Show Empathy**: Understand that selling a business can be an emotional process for the owner. Show empathy and acknowledge their feelings. This can help in building a stronger, more trusting relationship.

4. **Follow Up**: Consistency is key. Regular follow-ups show that you are serious about your interest. It also helps in keeping the conversation going and building a stronger connection over time.

Crafting Your Offer and Negotiation Tips

Making an offer is a critical step. Here's how to craft a compelling offer and negotiate effectively:

1. **Do Your Homework**: Before making an offer, gather all necessary information about the business. This includes financials, market position, and any potential risks. A well-informed offer shows that you are serious and prepared.

2. **Present** a **Win-Win Proposal**: Frame your offer in a way that benefits both parties. Highlight how the deal can provide value to the seller, such as maintaining the legacy of the business or taking care of existing employees.

3. **Be Flexible**: Flexibility can be a strong negotiating tool. Be open to different deal structures, such as seller financing or earn-outs. This shows that you are willing to work with the seller's needs and constraints.

4. **Negotiate with Confidence**: Approach negotiations with confidence but avoid being overly aggressive. State your terms clearly and be prepared to justify them. Confidence shows that you are serious and knowledgeable.

5. **Seek Win-Win Solutions**: The best deals are those where both parties feel they've gained something. Look for solutions that address the seller's concerns while meeting your needs.

6. **Get it in Writing**: Once an agreement is reached, make sure everything is documented. This prevents any misunderstandings and provides a clear record of what was agreed upon.

Approaching business owners requires a blend of effective communication, rapport-building, and smart negotiation. By following these strategies, you'll be well on your way to securing a successful deal. Keep these tips in mind as you engage with potential sellers, and you'll increase your chances of making a successful acquisition.

Financing Your Purchase

Different Financing Options

Financing a business purchase might seem daunting, but there are several options to consider:

1. **Seller Financing**: This is when the seller agrees to finance part of the purchase price. Instead of paying the full amount upfront, you make regular payments to the seller over time. It's a win-win: you get the business without needing all the cash upfront, and the seller continues to earn money.

2. **Loans**: Traditional bank loans are a common way to finance a business purchase. You'll need a solid business plan and good credit to secure a loan. The Small Business Administration (SBA) offers loans specifically for business acquisitions, which can be a great option if you qualify.

3. **Investor Partnerships**: Bringing in investors can help you finance the purchase. You offer them equity in the business in exchange for their financial support. This can be a great way to spread the financial risk and gain valuable business partners.

Creative Financing Strategies

If traditional financing methods aren't an option, get creative. Here are some strategies to consider:

1. **Sweat Equity**: Offer to work for the seller for a period of time in exchange for equity in the business. This allows you to invest your time and skills instead of cash.

2. **Earn-Out Agreements**: Agree to pay the seller a percentage of the business's future earnings. This ties the seller's payout to the performance of the business, reducing your initial financial burden.

3. **Asset-Based Lending**: Use the assets of the business, such as inventory or equipment, as collateral for a loan. This can provide the financing you need without requiring personal assets as collateral.

4. **Personal Savings** and **Retirement Funds**: If you have personal savings or retirement funds, you might consider using these to finance the purchase. Be cautious with this approach and consult with a financial advisor to understand the risks and tax implications.

Managing Cash Flow Post-Acquisition

Once you've acquired the business, managing cash flow is critical to ensure its success:

1. **Monitor Cash Flow Regularly**: Keep a close eye on your cash flow statements. Regular monitoring helps you identify trends and potential issues before they become major problems.

2. **Maintain** a **Cash Reserve**: Set aside a portion of your profits as a cash reserve. This provides a safety net for unexpected expenses and helps you manage cash flow during slower periods.

3. **Optimize Accounts Receivable** and **Payable**: Speed up collections from customers and negotiate longer payment terms with suppliers. This improves your cash flow by keeping more money in the business.

4. **Control Expenses**: Keep a tight rein on expenses. Regularly review your spending and look for areas where you can cut costs without sacrificing quality or service.

5. **Plan for Seasonal Variations**: If your business is seasonal, plan for the fluctuations in cash flow. Save more during peak seasons to cover expenses during slower periods.

6. **Invest in Growth Wisely**: Reinvest profits into areas that drive growth, such as marketing, new product development, or technology upgrades. Ensure these investments provide a good return and don't overextend your finances.

Financing your business purchase doesn't have to be a barrier. By exploring different financing options, getting creative with your strategies, and managing cash flow effectively post-acquisition, you can secure and grow your new business. Stay proactive, keep your finances in check, and focus on sustainable growth to ensure long-term success.

Due Diligence Process

Conducting Thorough Due Diligence

Due diligence is the critical process of investigating a business before you buy it. It's your chance to verify all the claims made by the seller and ensure you're making a wise investment. Here's how to conduct thorough due diligence:

1. **Financial Review**: Examine all financial documents, including profit and loss statements, balance sheets, and cash flow statements. Look for consistent revenue and profit trends and verify the accuracy of these documents.

2. **Operational Analysis**: Understand the day-to-day operations. This includes evaluating the business's processes, systems, and infrastructure. Assess the efficiency and effectiveness of current operations.

3. **Market Position**: Analyze the business's position in the market. Who are its main competitors? What is its market share? Understand the business's unique selling proposition and its competitive advantages.

4. **Customer** and **Supplier Relationships**: Review key customer and supplier contracts. Ensure these relationships are stable and long-term. Check for

any dependency on a few major customers or suppliers.

5. **Legal** and **Compliance**: Verify that the business complies with all relevant laws and regulations. Check for any pending or past legal issues, including lawsuits or regulatory violations.

6. **Employee** and **Management Review**: Evaluate the team. Who are the key employees, and what roles do they play? Assess the overall employee satisfaction and turnover rates.

Identifying Red Flags and Deal Breakers

During due diligence, keep an eye out for red flags that could indicate potential problems. Here are some common red flags and deal breakers:

1. **Inconsistent Financials**: Discrepancies in financial documents or unexplained fluctuations in revenue and expenses can be a major red flag.

2. **High Employee Turnover**: A high turnover rate might indicate issues with management or workplace culture.

3. **Legal Issues**: Ongoing or past legal problems, such as lawsuits or regulatory fines, can be deal breakers. Ensure there are no hidden liabilities.

4. **Customer Dependency**: If the business relies heavily on a few customers for the majority of its revenue, this poses a risk. Losing one of these customers could significantly impact the business.

5. **Outdated or Inefficient Operations**: Inefficiencies in operations, such as outdated technology or processes, can be costly to fix and hinder growth.

6. **Poor Market Position**: If the business is struggling to compete in its market or has a weak market share, it may not be a good investment.

Legal Considerations and Contract Essentials

Legal considerations are crucial in the due diligence process. Here are some key points to cover:

1. **Non-Disclosure Agreement** (NDA): Before you start due diligence, ensure that a non-disclosure agreement is in place. This protects both parties and ensures confidentiality.

2. **Purchase Agreement**: This is the main contract for the sale. It should detail the purchase price, terms of payment, and any conditions of the sale. Ensure it covers all aspects of the transaction and includes provisions for any contingencies.

3. **Employment Agreements**: If key employees are critical to the business, consider having employment agreements in place to ensure they stay on after the acquisition.

4. **Lease Agreements**: If the business operates out of leased premises, review the lease agreement terms. Ensure the lease is transferable and there are no hidden clauses that could affect your operations.

5. **Intellectual Property** (IP): Verify ownership of any intellectual property, such as trademarks, patents, or copyrights. Ensure that these assets will be transferred to you as part of the sale.

6. **Liabilities** and **Indemnities**: Clearly outline any liabilities that will be assumed by the buyer and any indemnities provided by the seller. This protects you from any unforeseen liabilities post-acquisition.

Conducting thorough due diligence, identifying red flags, and understanding legal considerations are essential steps in the business buying process. By taking these steps seriously, you can avoid costly mistakes and ensure that you are making a sound investment. Stay diligent, be thorough, and don't rush the process. Your due diligence will pay off in the long run.

Closing the Deal

Finalizing the Purchase Agreement

The purchase agreement is the final step in legally transferring ownership of the business. Here's how to ensure a smooth process:

1. **Review All Terms**: Carefully review all terms of the agreement with your lawyer. Make sure everything you've negotiated is included, and there are no hidden surprises.

2. **Confirm Financial Arrangements**: Ensure all financial details are accurate. This includes the purchase price, payment terms, and any financing arrangements.

3. **Sign the Agreement**: Once you're satisfied with the terms, both parties sign the agreement. This legally binds you to the purchase.

4. **Secure Funding**: Make sure your financing is in place. Whether it's a loan, seller financing, or investor funds, ensure the money is ready to transfer.

5. **Transfer of Ownership**: Arrange for the transfer of ownership. This includes changing ownership records with relevant authorities, transferring

business licenses, and updating any contracts or agreements.

Transition Planning and Integration

Transition planning is crucial for a smooth handover. Here's how to manage it effectively:

1. **Create a Transition Plan**: Develop a detailed plan outlining key tasks and timelines. This should cover everything from employee handovers to customer communications.

2. **Communicate with Stakeholders**: Inform employees, customers, and suppliers about the change in ownership. Clear communication helps maintain trust and continuity.

3. **Retain Key Employees**: If possible, retain key employees during the transition. Their knowledge and expertise can be invaluable.

4. **Maintain Operations**: Ensure that business operations continue smoothly during the transition. Avoid making major changes right away; focus on maintaining stability.

5. **Learn the Business**: Spend time learning the intricacies of the business. Understand its processes, systems, and culture before making significant changes.

Post-Acquisition Checklist

Once the deal is closed, it's time to focus on integrating and growing the business. Here's a checklist to guide you:

1. **Update Legal Documents**: Change the ownership details on all legal documents, including business licenses, leases, and contracts.

2. **Review Financials**: Go through the business's financials in detail. Set up your accounting systems and ensure everything is in order.

3. **Meet with Employees**: Hold meetings with employees to introduce yourself and outline your vision. Address any concerns they might have and reassure them about their roles.

4. **Engage with Customers**: Reach out to key customers to introduce yourself and ensure them of continued quality and service. Building strong relationships early on is crucial.

5. **Assess Operations**: Conduct a thorough review of business operations. Identify any immediate areas for improvement or optimization.

6. **Plan for Growth**: Develop a strategic plan for growing the business. Set clear goals and outline the steps needed to achieve them.

7. **Monitor Performance**: Regularly track the business's performance against your goals. Adjust your strategies as needed to stay on track.

8. **Maintain Cash Flow**: Keep a close eye on cash flow. Ensure you have enough reserves to cover any unexpected expenses and invest in growth opportunities.

9. **Seek Feedback**: Regularly seek feedback from employees, customers, and suppliers. Use their insights to make informed decisions and improvements.

10. **Stay Informed**: Keep up with industry trends and market conditions. Staying informed helps you make proactive decisions and stay ahead of the competition.

Closing the deal is a significant milestone, but it's just the beginning. By carefully finalizing the purchase agreement, planning the transition, and following a comprehensive post-acquisition checklist, you'll set yourself up for success. Stay proactive, keep communication open, and focus on integrating and growing the business smoothly. Your journey as a business owner is just beginning, and with the right approach, it will be a successful one.

Case Studies and Success Stories

Real-Life Examples of Successful Business Acquisitions

Let's dive into some real-life examples of entrepreneurs who successfully bought businesses and turned them into profitable ventures.

1. Jay's Journey to a Million-Dollar Business:
   a. Background: Jay worked for a company and always dreamed of owning her own business.
   b. The Acquisition: She learned that her coworker, who owned a business, was looking to retire. Jay proposed to buy the business using seller financing, meaning she would pay for the business over time from its profits.
   c. The Outcome: Jay successfully took over the business without any upfront cash. Today, her business generates over $1.5 million in annual revenue.

2. Ross's Expertise to Equity Deal:
   a. Background: Ross was skilled in online marketing but didn't own a business.
   b. The Acquisition: He partnered with a friend who ran an e-bike shop. Ross proposed to handle all online sales and marketing in exchange for 50% ownership of the business.
   c. The Outcome: Ross grew the online sales significantly, bringing in substantial revenue.

His innovative approach and expertise transformed the business into a profitable venture.

3. The Story of a Podcast Production Company
    a. Background: The founder of Strike Fire Productions loved running the operations but hated sales and marketing.
    b. The Acquisition: An investor noticed this gap and proposed to handle sales and marketing in exchange for equity.
    c. The Outcome: The business flourished under the new partnership, growing from a small operation to generating between $10,000 and $30,000 a month. Eventually, the investor sold his share back to the founder, making a significant profit.

Lessons Learned from Different Entrepreneurs

These success stories offer valuable lessons for anyone looking to buy a business:

1. **Be Persistent** and **Patient**: Jay's acquisition took time and persistence. She had to build trust with the owner and prove her worth. Patience paid off in securing a profitable business with no initial cash outlay.

2. **Leverage Your Skills** and **Expertise**: Ross turned his marketing expertise into a lucrative business deal. By focusing on what he was good at, he added value to the business and secured equity without needing significant capital.

3. **Identify** and **Fill Gaps**: The investor in Strike Fire Productions recognized that the founder needed help with sales and marketing. By addressing this need, he created a win-win situation that benefited both parties.

4. **Creative Financing Works**: Traditional financing isn't the only way to buy a business. Seller financing, sweat equity, and expertise-for-equity deals are all viable options. These creative strategies can help you acquire a business even if you don't have a lot of cash on hand.

5. **Understand the Business**: Each successful acquisition involved a deep understanding of the business being purchased. Whether it was Jay's familiarity with her coworker's business or Ross's expertise in online marketing, knowing the business inside out was crucial.

6. **Build Strong Relationships**: Trust and strong relationships were key in each of these stories. Whether with the seller, employees, or partners, building and maintaining good relationships helped ensure a smooth transition and successful business growth.

These case studies show that buying a business is not just about having the money; it's about persistence, creativity, and leveraging your unique skills and strengths. By learning from these successful entrepreneurs, you can gain valuable insights and inspiration for your own journey into business ownership. Stay focused, be innovative, and remember that there are many paths to success. Your dream business is out there, waiting for you to find and transform it.

Building and Growing Your Acquired Business

Implementing Growth Strategies

Once you've acquired a business, the next step is to grow it. Here's how you can implement effective growth strategies:

1. **Expand Your Customer Base**: Focus on attracting new customers while retaining your existing ones. Use marketing tactics like social media campaigns, email marketing, and special promotions to reach a wider audience.

2. **Diversify Your Product** or **Service Offerings**: Explore opportunities to introduce new products or services. This not only caters to a broader market but also reduces dependency on a single revenue stream.

3. **Improve Operational Efficiency**: Streamline operations to reduce costs and increase productivity. This can involve adopting new technologies, optimizing supply chains, or revising workflows to eliminate inefficiencies.

4. **Increase Online Presence**: In today's digital age, having a strong online presence is crucial. Invest in a professional website, engage with

customers on social media, and consider e-commerce options if applicable.

5. **Strategic Partnerships**: Form alliances with other businesses to expand your reach. Partnerships can help you access new markets, share resources, and enhance your offerings.

Managing Operations and Employees

Effective management of operations and employees is essential for the success of your business:

1. **Understand Your Operations**: Spend time learning every aspect of the business. Understand the processes, identify bottlenecks, and look for areas where you can make improvements.

2. **Empower Your Employees**: Your team is your greatest asset. Foster a positive work environment, provide training and development opportunities, and encourage open communication. Empower your employees to take ownership of their roles and contribute to the business's success.

3. **Set Clear Goals**: Establish clear, achievable goals for your business and communicate them to your team. Regularly review progress and adjust strategies as needed to stay on track.

4. **Maintain Quality**: Ensure that your products or services maintain high-quality standards. Customer satisfaction is key to building a loyal customer base and encouraging repeat business.

5. **Monitor Financial Health**: Keep a close eye on your finances. Regularly review financial statements, manage cash flow, and ensure that you are operating within budget. Make informed financial decisions to support sustainable growth.

Continuous Learning and Adaptation

In the ever-changing business landscape, continuous learning and adaptation are crucial:

1. **Stay Informed**: Keep up with industry trends, market changes, and new technologies. Subscribe to industry publications, attend conferences, and participate in relevant online forums.

2. **Seek Feedback**: Regularly seek feedback from customers, employees, and other stakeholders. Use this feedback to make informed decisions and improvements.

3. **Invest in Training**: Invest in ongoing training and development for yourself and your team. Continuous learning helps you stay ahead of the competition and adapt to new challenges.

4. **Be Flexible**: The ability to pivot and adapt is vital. Be open to change and willing to adjust your strategies as needed. Whether it's a shift in market demand or a new opportunity, flexibility can lead to growth and success.

5. **Network with Other Business Owners**: Join business groups, attend networking events, and connect with other entrepreneurs. Sharing experiences and learning from others can provide valuable insights and support.

Building and growing your acquired business requires a combination of strategic planning, effective management, and continuous learning.

By implementing growth strategies, managing operations and employees efficiently, and staying adaptable, you can drive your business towards long-term success. Stay proactive, keep learning, and always be ready to seize new opportunities. Your journey to growing a successful business is just beginning, and with the right approach, the sky's the limit.

Overcoming Challenges

Dealing with Initial Setbacks

Every business journey comes with its fair share of bumps and hurdles. Here's how to tackle those initial setbacks:

1. **Stay Resilient**: Entrepreneurship is about resilience. When you face setbacks, don't see them as failures but as learning opportunities. Analyze what went wrong, learn from it, and move forward.

2. **Seek Support**: Don't be afraid to ask for help. Whether it's advice from a mentor, insights from industry peers, or emotional support from family and friends, having a strong support system can help you navigate tough times.

3. **Adapt Quickly**: Be ready to pivot when things don't go as planned. Flexibility and the ability to adapt to changing circumstances are key to overcoming obstacles and finding new paths to success.

4. **Keep** a **Positive Attitude**: Maintaining a positive attitude can make a huge difference. Focus on the bigger picture and remind yourself why you started this journey in the first place. Positivity fuels perseverance.

Maintaining Motivation and Focus

Staying motivated and focused is essential, especially during challenging times:

1. **Set Short-Term Goals**: Break down your long-term vision into short-term, achievable goals. Celebrate small victories along the way to keep your motivation high.

2. **Create** a **Routine**: Establish a daily routine that keeps you productive and focused. Consistency helps build momentum and keeps you on track.

3. **Stay Organized**: Use tools like to-do lists, calendars, and project management software to stay organized. Clear organization helps you manage your time effectively and stay focused on your priorities.

4. **Take Care of Yourself**: Don't neglect your physical and mental health. Regular exercise, a healthy diet, and sufficient rest are crucial for maintaining high energy levels and a sharp mind.

5. **Surround Yourself with Positivity**: Build a network of positive influences. Engage with mentors, join supportive business communities, and keep away from negativity.

Long-Term Planning and Exit Strategies

Thinking ahead is crucial for sustained success and eventual exit:

1. **Develop** a **Long-Term Vision**: Have a clear vision of where you want your business to be in the future. Set long-term goals and outline the steps needed to achieve them.

2. **Regularly Review** and **Adjust Plans**: Business environments change, so regularly review your plans and adjust them as needed. Stay flexible and open to new opportunities.

3. **Build Value**: Focus on building value in your business. This includes strengthening customer relationships, improving operational efficiency, and enhancing your brand reputation. A valuable business is more attractive to potential buyers.

4. **Plan Your Exit Strategy**: Whether you plan to sell your business, pass it on to family, or merge with another company, having a clear exit strategy is crucial. Consider different scenarios and prepare for them in advance.

5. **Seek Professional Advice**: Consult with financial advisors, lawyers, and business brokers to help you plan your exit strategy. Their expertise can provide valuable insights and ensure you make informed decisions.

6. **Document Everything**: Keep detailed records of your business operations, financials, and key decisions. Proper documentation makes the transition smoother and more attractive to potential buyers.

Overcoming challenges, maintaining motivation, and planning for the long term are essential components of successful business ownership. By staying resilient, focused, and proactive, you can navigate setbacks, stay motivated, and build a valuable business that's ready for whatever the future holds. Keep pushing forward, stay adaptable, and always have an eye on the horizon. Your business journey is a marathon, not a sprint, and with the right strategies, you'll reach your goals and beyond.

Resources and Tools

Recommended Books, Websites, and Courses

Equipping yourself with the right resources is crucial for success. Here are some must-have tools for your journey:

1. **Books**:
   a. **"The Art of the Deal"** by Donald Trump: Learn negotiation tactics and business strategies from one of the most famous dealmakers.
   b. **"Buy Then Build"** by Walker Deibel: This book is a comprehensive guide on how to buy an existing business and scale it to new heights.
   c. **"The Lean Startup"** by Eric Ries: Though focused on startups, the principles of lean thinking and continuous improvement are invaluable.

2. **Websites**:
   a. **BizBuySell**: A leading online marketplace for buying and selling businesses. It offers a wealth of listings and resources.
   b. **SBA.gov**: The Small Business Administration's website provides essential information on loans, grants, and business management tips.
   c. **HubSpot Blog**: A treasure trove of articles on marketing, sales, and business growth.

3. Courses:
   a. **Udemy's "How to Buy a Business"**: An in-depth online course covering all aspects of business acquisition.
   b. **Coursera's "Entrepreneurship**: Buying and Selling a Business": Learn from top universities about the intricacies of business transactions.
   c. **LinkedIn Learning**: Offers various courses on negotiation, business strategy, and financial analysis.

Templates and Checklists

Templates and checklists can streamline your processes and ensure you don't miss any critical steps. Here are some essential ones:

1. **Personal Financial Planning Template**: Helps you keep track of your personal finances and ensure you're financially prepared to buy a business.

2. **Cash Flow Statement Template**: Essential for understanding the inflows and outflows of cash within the business, helping you avoid liquidity problems.

3. **Balance Sheet Template**: Provides a snapshot of the business's financial position, listing assets, liabilities, and equity.

4. **Profit** and **Loss Statement Template**: Allows you to see the business's revenues, costs, and profits over a specific period.

5. **Financial Projection Template**: Helps you forecast future revenues, expenses, and profits, which is crucial for planning and securing financing.

6. **Due Diligence Checklist**: Ensures you cover all bases when investigating a business before purchase, from financials to operations to legal considerations.

Networking and Support Groups

Building a strong network is invaluable. Here are some groups and communities to join:

1. **Chamber of Commerce**: Local chambers provide networking opportunities with other business owners and community leaders.

2. **Business Network International**: A global networking organization that helps businesses generate referrals and build strong relationships.

3. **LinkedIn Groups**:
    a. **"Small Business Network"**: Connect with other small business owners and share experiences and advice.

b. **"Business Acquisition** and **Mergers"**: A group focused on buying and selling businesses, offering valuable insights and opportunities.

4. **Facebook Groups**:
　　a. **"Entrepreneurs** and **Startups"**: A community for sharing tips, asking questions, and finding support from fellow entrepreneurs.
　　b. **"Small Business Owners"**: A group dedicated to the challenges and successes of running a small business.

5. **Industry-Specific Groups**: Join groups related to the industry of the business you're buying. These can provide specific insights, support, and networking opportunities.

Recap of Key Points

We've covered a lot of ground in this eBook, guiding you through the exciting journey of buying a business. Here are the key points to remember:

1. Understand the Basics: Know what business acquisition involves and why it's a great way to build wealth.

2. Mindset and Preparation: Develop the right mindset, overcome common fears, and set clear goals.

3. Finding Businesses to Buy: Explore different channels, utilize social media, and leverage your personal and professional networks.

4. Evaluating Business Opportunities: Understand key financial documents, assess business value, and stay informed about industry trends.

5. Approaching Business Owners: Communicate effectively, build rapport, and craft compelling offers.

6. Financing Your Purchase: Explore various financing options, get creative, and manage cash flow post-acquisition.

7. Due Diligence Process: Conduct thorough due diligence, identify red flags, and understand legal considerations.

8. Closing the Deal: Finalize the purchase agreement, plan the transition, and follow a post-acquisition checklist.

9. Case Studies and Success Stories: Learn from real-life examples and the lessons of successful entrepreneurs.

10. Building and Growing Your Acquired Business: Implement growth strategies, manage operations, and continually learn and adapt.

11. Overcoming Challenges: Deal with setbacks, maintain motivation, and plan for the long term.

12. Resources and Tools: Utilize recommended books, websites, courses, templates, and networking groups.

Encouragement and Next Steps

Embarking on the journey of buying a business is both thrilling and challenging. Remember, every successful business owner started where you are now taking that first step with determination and a willingness to learn. Here are your next steps:

1. **Take Action**: Don't just read about buying a business—take the plunge! Start searching for opportunities, reaching out to owners, and conducting your due diligence.

2. **Stay Persistent**: The road to business ownership is not without its bumps. Stay resilient, keep learning, and don't give up. Your persistence will pay off.

3. **Leverage Your Network**: Connect with mentors, join business groups, and seek advice from those who have been there before. Your network can provide invaluable support and guidance.

4. **Plan for Growth**: Once you acquire a business, focus on growth strategies and efficient management. Keep your eyes on the long-term vision and adapt as needed.

Final Words of Advice

Buying a business is one of the most rewarding paths to financial independence and personal fulfillment. As you move forward, keep these final pieces of advice in mind:

1. **Believe in Yourself**: Confidence is key. Trust in your abilities and stay positive, even when faced with challenges.

2. **Be Informed**: Knowledge is power. Stay informed about industry trends, market conditions, and best practices. Continuous learning will set you apart.

3. **Stay Flexible**: Be ready to pivot when necessary. Flexibility and adaptability are essential traits for any successful entrepreneur.

4. **Enjoy the Journey**: Remember to enjoy the process. The journey of buying and growing a business is filled with valuable experiences and opportunities for personal and professional growth.

Your journey to business ownership is just beginning. With the right mindset, strategies, and support, you have everything you need to succeed. Take the leap, embrace the challenges, and enjoy the rewards of being your own boss. The future is bright, and your business success story is waiting to be written. Go out there and make it happen!

Thank You for Your Purchase

Thank you for reading "**Don't Start a Business, Buy One**"! We hope you found the insights and strategies valuable on your journey to business ownership.

Your **feedback** is incredibly important to us. If you enjoyed this eBook and found it helpful, please take a moment to leave a review. Your review will help other aspiring entrepreneurs discover this resource and embark on their own successful business acquisition journeys.

Thank you for your support!

Best regards,
Elisabeth Miazello

Author Page

To leave a review on Amazon, just scan the code above or visit:

https://www.amazon.com/author/elisabeth.miazello

Also, By **Elisabeth Miazello**

Scan The Code Above to Visit Amazon.com

www.ingramcontent.com/pod-product-compliance
Lightning Source LLC
Chambersburg PA
CBHW070939220526
45469CB00007B/2442